A Rhyme for the Time

Dottie S. Pickering
and
James A. Andrews

Copyright © 2022 Dottie S. Pickering and James A. Andrews.

All rights reserved. No part of this book may be reproduced, stored, or transmitted by any means—whether auditory, graphic, mechanical, or electronic—without written permission of both publisher and author, except in the case of brief excerpts used in critical articles and reviews. Unauthorized reproduction of any part of this work is illegal and is punishable by law.

ISBN: 979-8-88640-538-5 (sc)
ISBN: 979-8-88640-539-2 (hc)
ISBN: 979-8-88640-540-8 (e)

Because of the dynamic nature of the Internet, any web addresses or links contained in this book may have changed since publication and may no longer be valid. The views expressed in this work are solely those of the author and do not necessarily reflect the views of the publisher, and the publisher hereby disclaims any responsibility for them.

THE EWINGS PUBLISHING

One Galleria Blvd., Suite 1900, Metairie, LA 70001
1-888-421-2397

January Winds

When January winds
Blow across my yard,
And snow piles up
And ice freezes hard,

I sit in my cozy chair
With my blanket and book,
All warm and happy
In my little nook.
M-m-m-m!

Snow

Snow, snow, snow,
Softly falling, fluffy.
Snow, snow, snow,
Bits of ice, sleet.
Packing snow, heavy, wet,
Will make a good snowman
I BET!

Eskimos

Eskimos kiss by rubbing noses,
Not like us, as one supposes;
They live in a land where it's mostly night,
And read their lessons by blubber light.

If I Were A Snowman

If I were a snowman, round and white,
I'd be the best looking one in sight.
With my colorful scarf and high-top hat,
Singing cold winter songs,
WHAT DO YOU THINK OF THAT??

Valentine Poem

Hearts and flowers,
Lace and candy,
Make a Valentine
That's dandy!
Say, "I love you",
"You're one of a kind."
"Please be my Valentine
If you don't mind."

Two Presidents

Washington and Lincoln,
Two great men,
Were our presidents
Way back then.

Washington was first,
Lincoln freed the slaves,
Both were great men
And very, very brave.

Groundhog Day

This is the day
The groundhog comes out.
Looks for his shadow
All about.

If he sees it
On the ground,
Old Man Winter's
Still around.
Br-r-r-r!

#1

Swans gliding gracefully,
Flower bouquets.
Beautiful hearts
And candy arrays.
Valentine's here
With all of its fun.
Just be my valentine
And you'll be #1.

Spring

Spring is here,
The flowers are out.
The birds are singing, the children shout . . .
"HURRAH FOR SPRING!"

St. Patrick's Day

Hi, I'm Paddy!
Poppin' in to say,
"Faith and begorra
And Happy St. Patrick's Day!"

Wearing Green

Be sure to wear green
On St. Patrick's Day,
Or elves and fairies
Will pinch away.

Wear the green
And dance the jig,
Find the shamrock
And you'll win big.

April

April is rainy,
April is nice.
To check the weather
You have to look twice.

Rainy and sunny,
Then showers will pour.
By the end of the month
You'll have flowers at your door.

Did You Know?

Did you know your slip is showing?
Or your shoestring is untied?
Better watch out,
It's April Fools
And tricks can't be denied.

Did you know it's time for flowers?
Lots of showers and the spring?
Take your umbrella
And your fella,
Go outside and sing.

Easter

Did you know it's Easter morning?
And our Savior rose to save?
Raise your voice and praise His glory,
He arose up from the grave.

Did you know that April brings showers?
That help the flowers along?
So many things to know about
The whole April month long.

In the Rain Forest

In the rain forest where the animals play,
And hunt for food both night and day,
They need our help to save their land,
So come on everyone and take a stand.
SAVE THE RAIN FOREST!

May

Here come the flowers,
Here come the trees,
Here come all things
That make us sneeze!

Beautiful flowers like
Petunias and roses,
All which contribute
To blowing our noses.
ACH-CHOO!

Vacation

Vacation is here
And we are glad,
We're tired of having
To subtract and add.

Swimming and ball games
And playing are fun;
We'll go out in the sun
And run and run.
SO LONG!

When It's June

When it's June
And I can see
All of summer
Spread out for me.

Ball games to play
Ice cream to eat,
Getting up late,
Boy, that will be neat!

Our Flag

Hurray for our flag,
All red, white and blue,
It stands for America
To whom I'm so true.

My country's the best,
I'm proud to live here.
I am an American,
Hear me cheer - - -
YEA, AMERICA!!

So Hot!

August heat waves,
No rain in sight,
Turn on the fans
Every night.

Intense heat,
Sweat on my brow,
Don't you think winter
Could come about now??
SO HOT!

Football

Fall is for football, teams and bands,
Selling hot dogs and cocoa in the stands.
Yell and cheer as the ball goes by,
If it reaches the goal post get ready to cry - - -
TOUCHDOWN!

A Little Man

There was a little man
Who planted apple trees,
Traveled barefoot all around
Made friends with birds and bees.

A tin pot was his hat,
In planting apples, he took the lead,
We have apples galore today
Because of - - -
JOHNNY APPLESEED!

Halloween Night

When the moon is a bright orange color,
And the bats fly 'round in fright,
You can count on something scary
Going BOO! On Halloween night.

Ghosts

Oh, we are the ghosts of Halloween!
Boo! Boo! Boo!
And whom do we haunt on Halloween?
You! You! You!
Indeed we are a spooky sight,
And we will moan and groan tonight,
And try to scare you with all our might!
Boo! Boo! Boo!

The Monster House

Come, come to the Monster House,
But be as quiet as a mouse.
Cause if they see you hangin' 'round,
They'll eat you up with a great big sound.
CRUNCH!

Pumpkins

Pumpkins ripening on the vine,
Pumpkins in the store;
Orange and plump and everywhere,
Sizes all galore.

Pumpkins all around my house,
Faces lit with glee;
Pumpkin pie, spicy and smooth
And it's all for ME!

Thanksgiving Day

Pilgrims and Indians together
With their harvest display,
Had a great big dinner
And called it Thanksgiving Day.

A Turkey Tongue Twister

Tom, Tom Turkey, tipped his hat
To two twin turkeys, who all sat
On the tip, tip, top of two tall tanks,
Saying prayers and giving thanks.

Tom told them a tale of a terrible time
When Tom's timid uncle towed the line.
He was tied and trussed and ready to trim,
Tom trounced the cook and rescued him.

Time is now, that Tom tells the tale
To tiny turkeys in the dale,
Teaches them to hide away,
And don't appear till AFTER Thanksgiving Day!

Christmas

Come one, come all,
It's that time of year,
When Santa Claus comes
With his sleigh and reindeer.
Thru the snowy night,
What a sight!

Santa

There is Santa,
Jolly and fat.
Dressed all in fur
And a red stocking hat.

Ho, ho, ho,
As he glides thru the night,
Bringing presents to all
He makes quite a sight.

Be sure to keep watch,
Keep your eyes open wide,
When he comes down the chimney
Jump out and cry - - -
HI SANTA!

Tiny Little Baby

Tiny little baby,
Born on Christmas night,
To shepherds and the Wise Men,
You were a glorious sight!

Angels sang around you,
A star hung overhead;
Just a tiny little baby,
And Oh, what joy you spread!

Christmas Bells

Christmas bells ring out the time,
"It's a brand new year!" they chime.
Make your resolutions now,
Keeping them, I don't know how!

A brand new year,
A brand new slate;
I'll write my life
Upon each date.
HAPPY NEW YEAR!

The Dinosaurs

Dinosaurs lived long ago,
Before the sleet, before the snow.
Lived in herds or lived alone,
The biggest animals we've ever known.

Some had spikes and some had claws,
Some had horns or bumps or paws.
Some were huge and some were small,
Some were short and some were tall.

They ate the plants,
And ate the meat,
On two hind legs
Or all four feet.

The dinosaurs died and are no more,
We only know how they were before,
By what the paleontologists find
From bones and eggs they left behind.

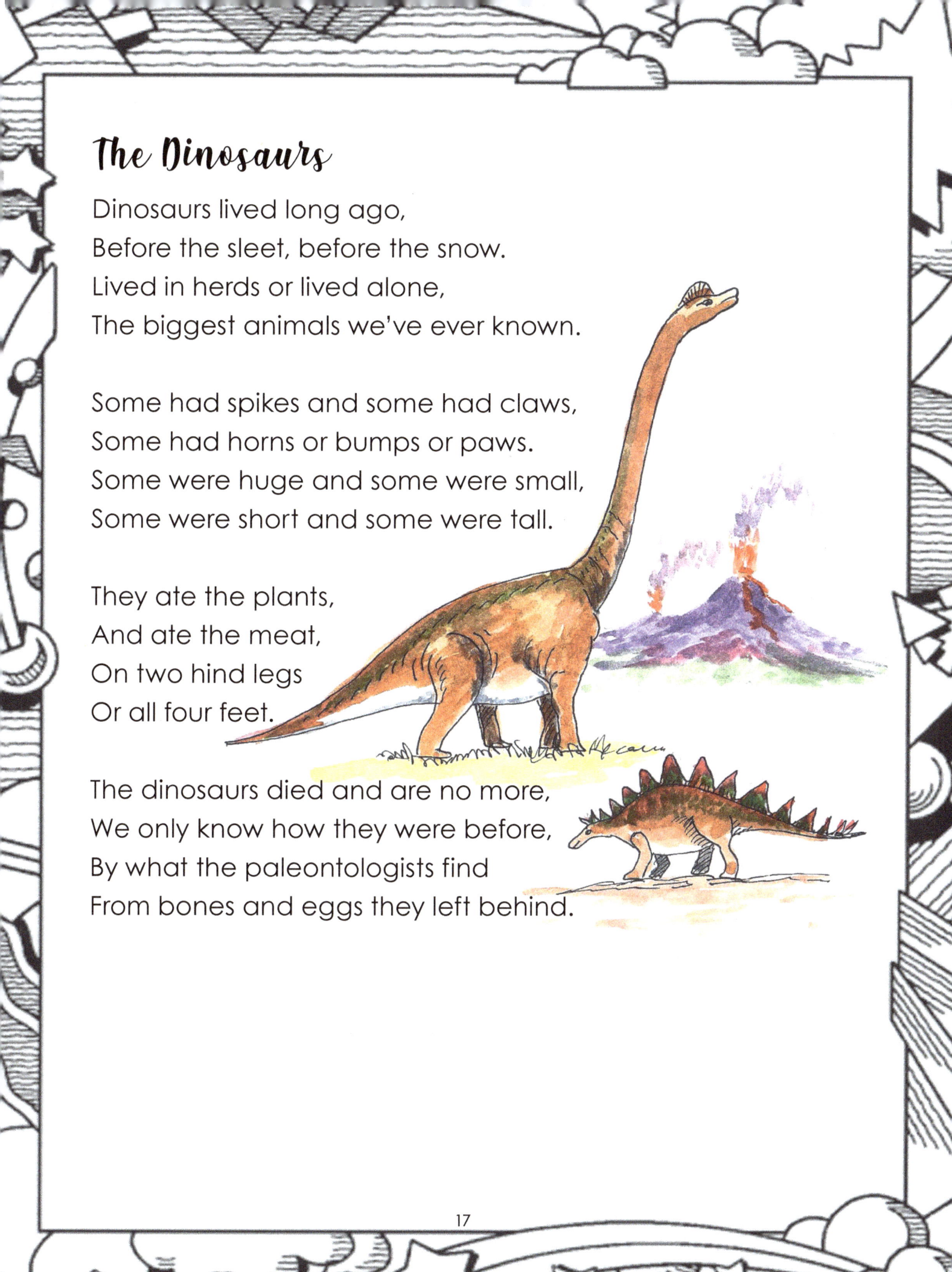

www.ingramcontent.com/pod-product-compliance
Lightning Source LLC
LaVergne TN
LVHW072131060526
838201LV00071B/5013